the Big Book of Bobbins

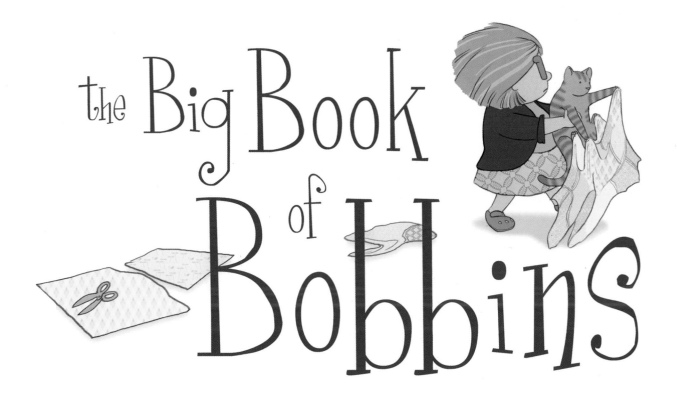

Fun, Quilty Cartoons by Julia Icenogle

To Aunt Camille, the real Mrs. Bobbins – j.i.

The Big Book of Bobbins
Fun, Quilty Cartoons by Julia Icenogle

Editor: Diane McLendon
Designer: Lon Eric Craven
Illustration: Julia Icenogle

Published by:
Kansas City Star Books
1729 Grand Blvd.
Kansas City, Missouri, USA 64108

First edition, first printing
ISBN: 978-1-935362-59-3

Library of Congress Control Number: 2010922707

Printed in the United States of America by Walsworth Publishing Co., Marceline, Missouri

To order copies, call StarInfo at 866-834-7467.

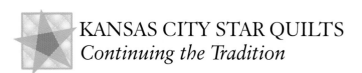

KANSAS CITY STAR QUILTS
Continuing the Tradition

Table of Contents

Introduction

Ask and you shall receive!

Since Mrs. Bobbins' inception on June 25, 2008, many quilters have become die hard Mrs. Bobbins fans. So much that they've asked for a Mrs. Bobbins book. Well here it is – The Big Book of Bobbins! It's 112 pages of Mrs. Bobbins' fun, silly, quilty antics!

The Big Book of Bobbins is divided into ten chapters – everything from quilting humor to quilting frustrations. You'll see Mrs. Bobbins use her rotary cutter on a pizza and accidentally sew her quilt to the tablecloth. You'll also get a glimpse at Mr. Bobbins' naivety when it comes to Mrs. Bobbins' hobby, then curiosity overwhelming him as he takes a stab at quilting himself! Enjoy the Holidays at the Bobbins' – always a quilty treat – and meet Mrs. Bobbins' friends and beloved cats. Top all of that off with current events and a road trip to a quilt show, and you have The Big Book of Bobbins!

But we must warn you: As you laugh through the pages, you may notice that Mrs. Bobbins reminds you off someone – YOU! Which may just be why so many of you have requested a book be made… [wink wink].

Diane McLendon
Editor

About Mrs. Bobbins

Mrs. Bobbins is a cartoon feature that appears weekly on Kansas City Star Quilts' blog www.PickleDish.com. In early 2008, as Kansas City Star Quilts was launching a new website, it decided it needed something fun that appeared every week so its readers had something to always look forward to. Kansas City Star Quilts hired quirky local artist Julia Icenogle, who came back a week later with the idea of Mrs. Bobbins, a lovable quilter with cats, quilting friends, and a "quilt-clueless" husband. Thus, on June 25, 2008, Mrs. Bobbins made her Internet debut! Since then, Mrs. Bobbins has appeared in calendars, on T-shirts, as decorative prints, and more. Visit www.PickleDishStore.com for more information.

meet  !

Mrs. Bobbins lives, breathes, and eats quilting …
and she has a lot to say about it!

She lives with her soft-spoken husband,
who is mystified by quilting …

… and her two overweight cats,
Patches and Fluffy, who always
seem to be in the way.

Her best friends and fellow quilters,
Alice, Edith, and Geraldine,
provide color and design advice …

… as well as a lot of good gossip.

Look for Mrs. Bobbins every week!

Quilt Humor

WHAT DID ONE QUILTER SAY TO THE OTHER?

Mrs. Bobbins loves jokes that
only quilters understand!

U.F.O.s
(Un-Finished Objects)

"Looks like your Aunt Bobbins sent
you another quilt postcard."

Mrs. Bobbins airs out her Flying Geese quilt.

Fussy Cut

Mrs. Bobbins finds religion.

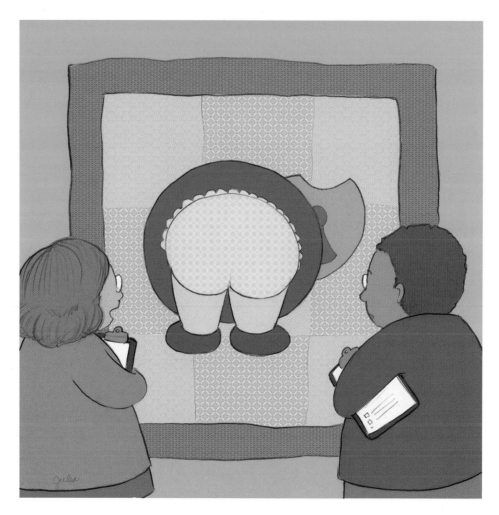

"I guess Mazel is still sore about last year's judging..."

One of the dangers of "brown bag quilting."

"I guess not all layer cakes work well wth candles."

One cool grandma.

"Basting the turkey. What does it look like I'm doing?"

Holidays

The Bobbins' go all out for the holidays, and somehow manage to make everything quilt-ily festive!

"Bar Gello? Is this some sort of
exclusive nightclub for quilters?"

Another exciting New Year's Eve at the Bobbins'.

Another New Year's Resoution bites the dust.

Father's Day at the Bobbins'

Picking Mrs. Bobbins out of a crowd
has always been really easy.

A week of late-night quilting has
Mrs. Bobbins ready for Halloween.

Another home hit by a growing
Halloween menace: quilt gangs.

The Bobbins' find out that quilt batting
is a poor substitute for turkey stuffing.

Camping out online for Cyber Monday is a lot easier than camping out in line for Black Friday

Piece on Earth

Every year as if by magic, the Guild's holiday party
Santa outfit appears, and Mr. Bobbins disappears.

"It could be worse…at least you're
not married to a scrapbooker."

Mr. Bobbins

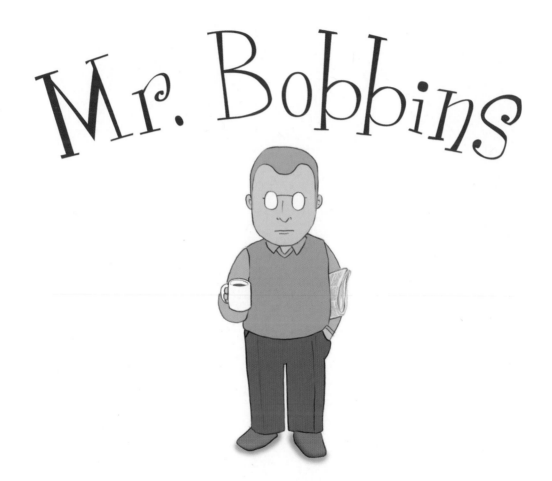

Mrs. Bobbins' DH. He just can't quite
wrap his mind around his wife's obsession.

"You know, their arms look pretty normal to me."

Mrs. Bobbins asks her husband
to bring her the rotary cutter.

"Mitered corners always do this to her."

"Oh. *THIS* fabric stash…"

"This isn't really what I had in mind when you asked if I wanted to see the fall colors."

"Oh, your quarters aren't that fat, dear."

"Laying out a quilt top over the mess
doesn't count as spring cleaning."

"People are starting to stare, Dear…"

Some people just aren't cut out for paper piecing.

Friends

Quilting is fun, but it's triple the fun
when good friends are involved!

Quilters Anonymous

Stitch in the Ditch Club

The Quilt 'n' Quaff Club never actually got around to quilting. Not that anyone cared.

Quilters' Poker

Mrs. Bobbins likes the challenge
that her cats bring to her quilting.

"What do you have that will
look good with cat hair on it?"

"This has got to be the worst possible time for a hot flash."

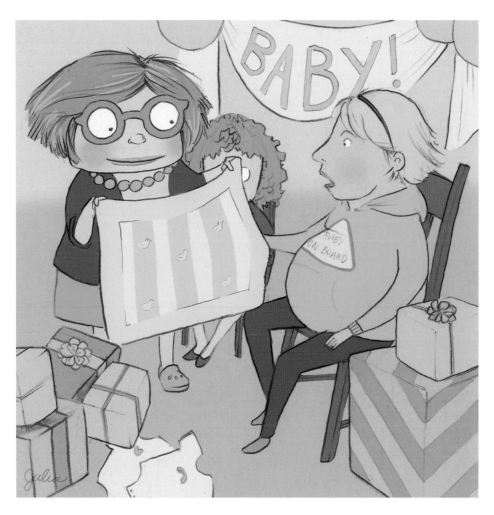

"Well, I guess cat hair is *technically* a natural fiber…"

Batting Battles

"Dear, next time you're spray basting in here,
lock the cat up in another room."

"Careful, Fluffy. Unlike you,
this machine still has its claws ."

World Events

Mrs. Bobbins likes to keep up on what's happening in the world, and sometimes a little quilt flair sneaks in!

"3 minutes, 23 seconds…and she's
on pace to shatter the Olympic record!"

Doing her part to stimulate the economy, Mrs. Bobbins engages in another wild night of online shopping.

"I'll vote for any candidate that supports
my right to carry a concealed seam ripper."

The year the Quilt Guild was in charge
of the Westridge precinct.

"YES, WE DID!"

Quilt Show

Mrs. Bobbins and pals head to the
Selvage County Fair for a quilty adventure!

As the deadline approached for the Selvage County Fair,
the quilt show night terrors begin to set in.

Quilt Show Panic, Stage Two: The All-Nighter

"Geraldine, when you said you would finish
your quilt on the way to the show,
I had assumed you'd be further along than that…"

"Hang on, everyone! My GPS just
alerted me to a new quilt shop"

The ladies visit the Holy Land.

When it comes to over-buying at the factory outlet, resistance is futile.

"Why, yes, we *are* here for the quilt show!
How did you ever guess?"

"Aren't you glad we quilted our own name tags?
We are really going to stand out!"

"I would complain, but to be honest, I think the low lighting will work to my advantage."

Mrs. Bobbins subtly tries to
influence the quilt show judges.

"Stand back, Geraldine…I'm popping the hatch
and this baby's packed tighter than a black hole."

Mr.Bobbins, Act II

Curiousity kills the cat…
err, Mr. Bobbins.

In a moment of weakness, Mr. Bobbins
considers reading the quilt magazine,
little knowing the power he was about to unleash.

Pattern in hand, Mr. Bobbins takes
his first solo journey into a quilt shop.

As it turns out, engineers
make good quilters. Who knew?

For Mr. Bobbins, the risk of being
discovered was part of the thrill of quilting.

Mr. Bobbins avoids discovery with the old
trains-in-the-basement ruse.

A complicated quilt pattern has Mr. Bobbins calling for help. Unfortunately, the hotline connects to his wife's cell phone.

Mr. Bobbins' secret quilt is discovered.

The problems of a two-quilter household.

Life

For Mrs. Bobbins, even when quilting isn't
on her mind, it seems to pop up everywhere!

"I probably should have started this swimsuit project earlier in the year."

"This pattern is called
'Double Wedding Ring With Prenup.'"

While Mr. Bobbins was away on business,
Mrs. Bobbins took the opportunity
to work on her favorite quilting project.

"If I have to spend $16 on a rotary cutter,
it had better cut more than just fabric!"

Mrs. Bobbins finds out how much
her charm quilt vest looks like honeycomb.

I can tell you're a quilter
by the threads on your shirt.

Mrs. Bobbins' piecing skills tend to
show up in unexpected places.

"I see you found my scraps.
Nice piecing, by the way."

"Quilting or non?"

Frustrations

Even though Mrs. Bobbins loves to quilt,
it does have its frustratingly funny moments.

"Shoot, I think I've quilted in the tablecloth again."

"When you're finished, I need you to shave this old quilt…it's bearding, too."

"The moths that eat my wool quilts
get appliquéd over the holes they make."

"I'm telling you, Edith, carpal-tunnel just proves that I deserve a big blue ribbon!"

"Here's a little something to help my quilt get to the top of the queue…and no questions asked."

Mrs. Bobbins learns the hard way
always to buy extra fabric for the binding.

Overnight guests at the Bobbins' may not
be able to breathe, but they are never cold.

"It *is* a little bit late for Christmas peppermints.
Let's say they're beach balls."

A little microquilting goes a long…
actually, it only goes a little way.

"I've been fighting this windmill so long
I feel like Don Quixote."

Until Next Time!

About Julia Icenogle

Julia Icenogle is the quirky artist behind Mrs. Bobbins and her hilarious antics. She draws inspiration from her aunt – the "real Mrs. Bobbins," as Julia refers to her. Julia tried to make a quilt once, but her beloved dog Marta promptly scattered the pieces everywhere, so Julia decided to stick to pencil and paper for her creative outlet. She is, however, "beginning to see quilt patterns in everyday life, just like Mrs. Bobbins!"

Julia is currently working toward her master's degree in Occupational Therapy. Twice a week, she volunteers at Alphapointe Association for the Blind, where she also helps with an arts and crafts day every other weekend. She is also training Marta, her quilt-destroying dog, to become a certified therapy dog.

Julia spends most of her free time doodling, gazing longingly at pretty fabric, and going to the dog park. You can check out her work at **www.ironnailcreative.com.**

Don't forget to check out other Mrs. Bobbins merchandise!